Tail Gunner

The
Leonard E. Thompson
Story

Leonard E. Thompson
Graduation photograph
USAAF Gunnery School

Tail Gunner

The Leonard E. Thompson Story

Compiled and Edited by

Charles M. Province

A CMP Scholastic Book
Published by CMP Productions

Scholastic Services Division

Copyright 2010 by Charles M. Province
All Rights Reserved

Other Books by
Charles M. Province

Pure Patton
Patton's Third Army
The Unknown Patton
Patton's Punch Cards
Patton's One-Minute Messages
Patton's Third Army in World War II
Walton Walker: The Man Who Saved Korea

This book is dedicated to my friend Gertrude Thompson and to all the men Leonard served with aboard B-17s in the 401st Bombardment Group.

Staff Sergeant Leonard E. Thompson
401st Bombardment Group
Tailgunner

Table of Contents

True Tales of a B-17 Tail Gunner...........................11

The 401st Bombardment Group............................35

A History of the B-17 42

An Informal Photo Album 49

Preface

This short history of Leonard Thompson's adventures as a B-17 Tail Gunner comes from various sources. It is partly from a short narrative written by Leonard himself, from videotapes of him telling stories to friends and family, from books and internet sources depicting the history of both the B-17 and the 401st Bombardment Group, and lastly from discussions with Leonard's friends and family.

I have used as much original material as I could find to piece together this small volume as a tribute to the courage and heroism displayed by Leonard during World War II. I have done my best to retain the personality and valor of Leonard in my editing of this book. If there are mistakes in this small volume, I take full responsibility for them and apologize in advance.

Anyone who ever met Leonard liked him immediately. His friends and family thought of him as reliable, funny, and above all a sincerely good man. During my interviews, I was told by many people that Leonard was never heard to say anything bad about anybody. I also heard about Leonard and his sense of humor; such as the time he received an unsolicited phone call from a cable company extolling their services and programming. Leonard listened quietly, agreeing with everything the salesperson told him and when it came time to "sign up" Leonard said, "That all sounds wonderful. I'd really like to do it if I weren't blind." Then there was the time he invited one of his friends over to help him fix his malfunctioning garage door. The friend kept trying to work the garage door opener and sometimes it worked, sometimes it didn't.

Finally he opened the hand-held device to look inside and he said, "Hey, there aren't even any batteries in here. There's no way it can work." Leonard opened the door again with the remote control hidden in his bib overalls and his friend realized he had been had by the ultimate practical joker.

To give the reader an idea of Leonard's sense of humor, I've included something he wrote, using it as the introduction to this book. It displays Leonard's unique approach to humor.

I have come to the conclusion that Leonard was what is called an "old soul." By that I mean he was a person wise beyond their years, with strong emotional stability, having a special understanding of the world around them, and possessing more wisdom than the average person.

When Leonard was eleven, his father died and he felt it was his responsibility to take care of his family. After entering the army during World War II, he always sent home most of his money. He was as hardworking and reliable as a man can be. Leonard and his fiancé, Gertrude, had to wait to get married because he wanted his sisters to all be married and settled before he did so. Leonard always took car of his family.

What I have tried to do here, is to edit and formulate a readable and true history of Leonard's time as a B-17 Tail Gunner. Leonard was a full-fledged member of the "greatest generation." He was a hero and he deserves to be remembered. As long as he is remembered, he will never truly die.

Charles M. Province
Oregon City, Oregon
2010

Introduction

The Guy Up Front

By

Leonard E. Thompson

"Tail Gunner to pilot." Over.

"This is the pilot." Over.

"Tail Gunner to pilot. I have a problem back here. Like my guns don't shoot straight and my heater suit won't keep me warm and the relief tube is too far away and much too cold to use anyway. My earphones don't work very well and I have a hard time hearing you and I need a much lighter flak suit because this one is heavier than it was before. My parachute harness is getting too tight and I was looking at the escape and the door sure looks small and my windows must be going haywire because they are hard to see out of. The cover on the tail wheel must be bad because a lot of cold air comes in that I don't remember from before and if I can get all these things fixed, this old Tail Gunner might have a few more miles left in him." Over.

"Pilot to Tail Gunner. Join the club, Pal." Over.

Chapter One

True Tales of a B-17 Tail Gunner

World War II was in full swing when I graduated from Oregon City High School in 1943 and at the age of 17, I was too young to go into the armed forces. But, a few months later, that was a different story.

On December 21st, 1943 I was loaded onto a bus with a bunch of friends I had graduated with and we were out to see the world.

Day one was very busy. We were issued clothes and a cot to sleep on. The next few days consisted of taking examinations and various types of tests. On Christmas day it was my turn to learn all about "kitchen police" and things like peeling spuds and washing dishes. I must have flunked one of those tests because the next day I was on a train and on my way to Denver, Colorado for more tests. They told me I had exceptional eyesight for some reason and that I would make a great gunner on a B-17. I think they just needed warm bodies to replace bomber casualties.

Two days later, I was on my way to Boulder City just outside of Las Vegas, Nevada for gunnery training. At this point, I was officially in the Army Air Force and it wasn't too bad being out in the desert. I saw a lot of Road Runners (they're birds like the ones in the cartoons) for the first time and they were everywhere.

It was here that I had my first airplane ride. We flew in a small two-seater with an open cockpit and we shot at targets on the ground. There was also a "ball turret" mounted on a flatbed railroad car that we used for mechanical fire training. We must have flown all over that desert just shooting at ground targets.

We were put into the back of a pickup truck and were driven around in a zigzag course shooting at clay pigeons. It was very much like trap shooting with a 12-gauge shotgun. After shooting over a hundred rounds on my first day, my shoulder was really sore. After a few days of that, we were on a train again and on the way to Rapid City, South Dakota.

On our first night there, I was introduced to what real wind and snow is like. When we got up the next morning, the snow was up to the windows on the second story but the other side of the building was almost bare. The wind had howled all night. What a learning time that was.

Here at the home of Mount Rushmore, I finally climbed aboard my first B-17 Flying Fortress. We did more target shooting and we got very good at hitting what we were aiming at. One day on the gunnery range, some farmer's sheep wandered among our targets and I'll be darned if some of them didn't get shot. It turned out to be pretty bad for us, though, since we ended up eating mutton for a week. We told ourselves we wouldn't be doing that again.

Our next training operation was night flying and we bombed targets with a camera. It was during one of these night operations that we experienced our first mechanical problems with the B-17. We were coming in for a landing, our wheels failed to lock down, and we sailed all the way down the runway with sparks flying everywhere. The guy in the control tower began yelling over the radio for us to get off the runway so the next plane could come in. I thought to myself, "Now there's a really alert air traffic controller."

We got into town a couple of times while at Rapid City and we were very surprised to see all the attractive Indian girls with those big, dark eyes. But, there was no time for that. We were on the move again.

After another train ride we were on the east coast. Then we were on a troop ship crossing the Atlantic Ocean and dodging German submarines. The troop ship was small, the ocean was large, and the trip was very, very rough. Almost all of the soldiers aboard were seasick.

The so-called "bathroom" on the ship was nothing but a big room with a couple of trenches with running water and a handrail. It took a time or two before I was able to master squatting across the trench, hanging onto the rail, and doing the paperwork.

We had better luck with eating because the ship's crew was French and our radio operator spoke French. We were invited into the kitchen and given some very good food that wasn't available to the rest of the soldiers.

When it came to sleeping, though, it was a bit more tricky. Our bunks were stacked eight high and the only way to the top bunk was by climbing all the way up over the other seven guys. It seemed to me like the guy on the top always had to get out and go to the bathroom a lot. And if he got sick, it was no fun for the other guys below him.

After a week of troop ship living, we were finally walking down the gangplank onto English soil. We were all pushed onto a bus and then we were on our way to our "home away from home" which turned out to be a Quonset Hut with a coal stove in the center and single cots for a dozen soldiers.

The out houses were back of the hut and POWs were given buckets and the job of cleaning them every couple of days. Although it sounds like an awful job, they were happy to have a roof over their heads, to have lots to eat, and to be away from the fighting and killing. When you think about it, they had it made.

On the very first night we were in England, the air raid siren went off and we all ran to the Air Raid

Shelter. A little while later, the "all clear" blast was sounded and we were all back to our beds but sleep was far from easy.

The funny thing was that I never had to go through basic training like a lot of soldiers did. I guess they must have really needed crews for the B-17s and that's why I was rushed through everything and ended up in England so quickly.

In the next months, we flew to Giessen, Nurnburg, Harburg, Siegen, Hagen, Hopsten, Barmingholten, Rheine, Unterluss, Royan, Merseburg, Harburg, Frankfurt, Eschweller, Misburg, Berlin, Kassel, Rheinback, Cologne, Dresden, Ludwigshafen, and many, many more targets with names I could not pronounce.

On my first raid, I found a penny and kept it with me. After we returned home safely, I figured that this must be a lucky penny so I drilled a hole in it, put it on the chain with my dog tags, and I've kept it ever since.

On one raid to Berlin we were hit with very heavy and very accurate flak. We also took a lot of Me109 fighter shells. We came back with 127 bullet holes in our airplane. Two of them were big enough for me to crawl through. I was amazed that not a single person got hurt during this raid and there was no vital damage to our plane. On another raid, our landing gear was shot up so badly we had to land without wheels. The plane took a real beating and it didn't look too good when we crawled out afterward.

Our second trip to Berlin went just like it always did. We were briefed at 0315 hours and we learned that our target was the Railroad Marshaling yards there. By 0700 hours we were airborne and on our way to drop some destruction. On this trip we were carrying "hundred pound bombs" and "incendiary bombs." Incendiary Bombs were not meant to blow things up, but to set fire to everything.

When we reached Berlin, we were once again met with very accurate flak but we saw something new.

We were attacked by Me-262 jet fighters, the first of their kind that I had ever seen. The Me-262 fighters met us and attacked from six o'clock, hiding in our contrails. As they pressed the attack, I got a really good look at them as they came straight at me. I almost ran out of shells. During this raid, our group lost fifteen planes and eight more were very badly damaged.

On our bombing mission to Giessen, we were hit hard and suffered some real bad damage. We kept losing altitude and we only made it as far as the English Channel, where we had to ditch the plane in that icy water. When we stopped bouncing, we all got out as quick as we could because the plane is only supposed to float for a short amount of time before sinking. The theory was that we should all get out onto the wing and into the lifeboats from there. Well, it sounded good on paper, I guess. The problem was that when we jumped into the lifeboats, it was like a trampoline and we bounced out and into the water where we went straight down. Luckily we had our Mae West life jackets on and we popped up like a cork on a fishing line. We all made it out of the plane and into the lifeboats and we were very lucky that a boat came along about thirty minutes later and picked us up. That was the first time I rode down with a damaged B-17 on a bombing mission.

Another rough mission was the one over Cologne. After losing two engines we were unable to keep up with our group. We were losing altitude and we all knew we were in real trouble. The pilot (Charles Bennett) gave us the option of either bailing out or riding the plane down. I had ridden it down before so I stayed with the pilot. The rest of the crew bailed out and they were never seen again.

The pilot said it was going to be a rough landing since our landing gear was shot up again. He told me to get into "crash position" which was in the radio room with my back against the wall, sitting down and looking backwards. I kept my hands "locked" behind the head. Boy, was he ever right when he said "rough landing." We hit the ground hard and we bounced around a lot before coming to a stop. We crash landed in France but it was occupied by German troops.

Now, the first thing to be done after a crash landing (if you can walk away from it) is to get out of the plane and run like hell because most of the time the plane would blow up. I got out and ran for the woods. Within a few seconds I heard a loud "boom" and I knew the pilot had not been able to escape from the cockpit.

I thought to myself, "God bless his soul." He had saved my life but lost his. As I ran along, I had my army issue Colt .45 automatic in my right hand and I kept getting closer to the woods.

I saw a man (a farmer) standing by a tree watching me and I was wondering if he might have a gun behind the tree. He waved at me and when I got closer he put out his hand to shake hands. When I got close enough to make sure he had no gun bur really wanted to shake hands, I put my .45 in my left hand and shook his hand.

Now, of course, he spoke French and I only spoke English but he motioned for me to follow him. We soon came to an old barn and we both went inside. He put up both hands indicating that I was to "stay where I was" and he left. I crawled into the hay and it soon became dark. Later on, he came back and wanted to shake hands again and he tugged on my arm, wanting me to follow him. "Boy, what am I getting into," I thought to myself. It was only a short walk before we came to a house, still in the woods, and very dark.

He led the way inside and the only light in the house was from a small candle. There was a bubbly old woman who must have been his wife. She gave me a bowl of soup and a glass of milk. He took me outside again and showed me the outhouse and then took me back inside the house to a small room in the back. He moved a rug and there was a trap door going under the house. He climbed under the floor and once more tugged on my arm wanting me to follow him.

Now, all of this was done in the dark and the only light we had was that single, small candle. What I saw under the floor was a couple of blankets and a bucket to pee in. There were also a few matches and another small candle in the small area. When he started to leave, he shook my hand again and then he was gone. The trap door was closed.

Now I felt trapped and began to think all kinds of things. There was just enough room to sit up without bumping your head but I was tired so I laid back and must have gone to sleep.

The next thing I knew, the trap door was opening. I was wide-awake in about two seconds and I grabbed my .45. But it was just the farmer and his wife again with a bowl of mush, a glass of milk, and a thick chunk of bread with lots of butter on it. Another handshake and the trap door closed again.

A few hours later I was given another chunk of bread, lots of butter, a glass of milk and another handshake.

Much later, the door opened again and the farmer came down with a small candle and he pointed at the pee bucket and waved for me to go with him to the outhouse where I dumped my bucket. He led me back into the house and his jolly old wife fed me some soup, more bread and butter, and another glass of milk. By now I was figuring they must have a cow hidden somewhere. Once more it was time to go back into hiding under the house. At lease it was much warmer under the house than it was outside.

We all followed this routine for three nights and on the fourth day, the French underground showed up to take me someplace. I started to buckle on my gun but the guy surprised me by speaking English and telling me, "No, it might cause you to be recognized." So I gave my gun to the farmer and he seemed to be very happy with the present. His wife had tears in her eyes and I think I did, too.

The guy from the underground gave me a funny looking hat and coat to wear and we were out the door and on our way to "who knows where."

It was almost dark by the time we got to an old dock in the harbor where we went down some rickety steps and met two more American soldiers. He took the coat and hat from me and told us all to stay where were. He said a boat would be along very soon. The three of us were surprised when a little rowboat showed up and the guy rowing the boat told us all to get in. Now, with him and the other three of us in this "itty bitty" boat he started rowing. I knew we could never cross the English Channel in this thing without going under. But, he kept rowing in the dark and about thirty minutes later we came upon a much larger boat.

On the larger boat, the captain said we had to wait for air cover before we could leave. Just then the radio made a funny sound and he said it was okay now and that we had air cover. So, out into the English Channel we went and all I can say is that it was a really rough trip.

At just about daylight, we were back in England. We were taken to a mess hall and we were given a big meal and then put into a truck that was taking supplies to some of the airbases.

By the time it was dark that evening, I was back at my base and in my own bed. Well, it wasn't my own original bed and all of the other beds of the rest of my crew were also gone. Everything had been cleaned out while I was away.

Later, I went to the office and after a long briefing my things showed up and a new room was assigned to me. After a week or two, I was back on duty with a new crew. I was flying again.

Sometimes I still choke up when I realize that I

was the only survivor out of a crew of ten men. I can still see their faces if I think about them and I especially think about the pilot and how he died.

When I was hiding under the farmer's house in France, I left my parachute and my "Mae West" life jacket there. I sometimes wonder if they're still there and where that Colt .45 automatic is. Are they still there and all rusty or are they hanging up on the wall of that old farmhouse which was my "home away from home" for a few days. I also wonder if there were other servicemen helped by that farmer and his jolly old wife.

On a later mission, I remember our radio operator getting his leg shot off and his bleeding to death. The guys in charge had to get us a new "first time" radio operator and we were off again. Down the runway we went. We just barely got airborne when two of our motors cut out and we had to make a crash landing.

Because we had a full load of bombs and we were very heavy, the plane didn't have enough brakes to stop us in time and we ended up in a cornfield. The truck came out and picked us up and put us on another plane but the "new guy" cracked up and went nuts. He refused to fly. So we ended up having to wait until yet another radio operator was found to round out our crew. By the time a replacement was found, it was too late in the day and we were unable to catch up with the rest of our airborne group so we ended up with the rest of the day off.

When we finally were ready for the next mission, we flew lead plane but instead of having a ball turret, we had radar in its place. With radar, we could see to bomb in almost any kind of weather.

With the radar controlling our bomb run, we would get close to our target, the bomb bay door would open, and the bombardier would drop a smoke bomb. This signal alerted the rest of the planes in the group that we were approaching the target. When we dropped our bombs the rest of the group dropped theirs, too. With our planes grouped close together all those bombs did an awful lot of damage in a small area.

I remember one time when a bomb would not release and the top turret gunner went to kick it loose. When it finally let go, he fell out with it and he wasn't wearing his parachute. I can still remember hearing him as he fell. His last words were, "Well, damn me."

All the bombs we dropped had safety tags with color keys and to make the bomb live you had to pull the cotter pins out after you were in flight. That was part of my job. I saved a tag and cotter pin from each mission we flew and wrote on the tag what our target was, how many bombs we dropped, how high we flew, and how cold it was. Most likely the average temperature would be between minus 32 and 54 degrees. In a drafty place like a bomber airplane, that was mighty cold. When you go above 10,000 feet you have to wear an oxygen mask and the moisture from your breath will freeze, causing icicles all the way down your jacket.

After dropping our bombs and leaving the target areas we always went through lots of flak. It was always a shock to look around and see new holes in your plane that weren't there before. But, on the bright side, at least there weren't any bumble bees up there to fly in and sting you.

A few times, when we crossed the English Channel and flew over Belgium, we would see the German V2 rockets take off, go way up and over, and then crash onto English soil. One time Gordon Cupp (our top gunner) and I were on leave in London seeing the sights when a V2 hit very close to us. The concussion picked us both up and tossed us about twenty to thirty feet away. But we didn't get hurt too badly. We did see a horse that had been hit and it was an ugly sight. The funny thing is that we heard very little noise. We never went back again to "see the sights." We had seen plenty of sights by then.

At our main base, our Quonset Hut always seemed to have lots of holes in the ceiling. The reason was rats. When rats would run across the ceiling joist, some of the guys would have target practice. The .45 automatic was not standard issue for enlisted men, but with a carton of cigarettes, you could buy just about anything you wanted. Since I didn't smoke, my ration box filled up fast. Most of the time, I'd give them away but sometimes there were things I could use.

On one mission, I remember we were hit extra hard by flak, which would ricochet all over the inside of the plane. I got hit in the leg once and still have the scars on my right shin.

As the war progressed, our targets got further and further away. Often, when the target would be too far away from our base to make a round trip, we would drop our bombs and fly to Russia to land, fuel up, and reload with more bombs. We would stay overnight and make the return trip the next day. If you want to live where it's always cold, just move to Russia. Man, it's always cold there.

Before we reached our targets, we would always throw out our chaff, which looked like the shiny tinsel used on Christmas trees. That was to make it look like millions of airplanes on the German radar but it never took long for them to figure out what was what and who was who.

One time the Germans fighters set themselves way out from us and shot rockets at our formation. We could see the big balls of fire coming at us and we tried to get out of the way. Maneuvering like this caused our group to break up for a short time and the Me109 fighters would try to pick off the planes that got too far away from our concentrated firepower. This was very smart. It was like wolves preying on the weak animals in a herd. Sometimes, when we were under heavy attack from Me109's we would see a German plane out of range flying alone.

It was these guys who were reporting to the German fighters which target might be the best for them to pick on (again, very smart).

One time, I remember, when we were high over Germany, I had to go potty really bad but on our planes we didn't have an inside toilet. Well, the problem is that when you have to go, you have to go. I took off my flak helmet, filled it up, and tossed the helmet (and everything in it) out of the tail wheel cover. I guess you could say I really crapped on the enemy that time.

When we made it back over the English Channel, the oxygen masks could be taken off. The White Cliffs of Dover were always a welcome sight. By this time, our base would be in sight and we would fire a red flare if we had wounded men on board. This would give us a priority landing with the ambulance following you to the landing pad.

Safely back on earth, we would gather up our gear, get into the back of a "lorry" (a truck), and we would be on our way back to our hut where we would clean up and ride our bikes over to the mess hall. It seemed to me like we always missed lunch. Also, when flying at high altitude for eight hours or more and being on oxygen most of the time, you get very tired.

After lunch, we would check the bulletin board to see if we were scheduled for duty the next day and, if not, we'd get a good night's sleep.

By this time, the ground crew would already be working fast and furious to patch up all those holes left in the B-17 by flak and enemy fighters. They also had to find and clean out all the empty shell casings. They would restock the plane with live shells, bombs, gas, etc. Everyone had a job to do and they do it without questions.

When you're eighteen years old, you do a lot of growing up fast, and you just look ahead to the next flight.

On April 12, 1945, our Commander-in-Chief

(Franklin D. Roosevelt) died and soon after, the war in Europe was over. VE Day (Victory in Europe Day) was announced on the 8th of May, 1945.

A month later, we were all flying our planes home via Iceland and Greenland, then on to the U.S.A. We were told we would be transferring to the Pacific Theater and fighting the Japs. But then, we heard some good news. The war had also ended in Japan. When we heard the news, we were in New York City, waiting to catch a train on the way to Albuquerque, New Mexico.

While waiting for the train, three black boys started to give us a bad time for some reason. That was a big mistake on their part. I waded into them and without a worry in the world made an awful mess of them. The last I saw of them was as they were dragging one another away. That made me feel good. After everything I had just been through in the war, I had grown up in a hurry. When the fight was over, David Gross, the gunner, was laughing. He asked, "Do you need any help?"

When we had gotten back to the states and were finally heading home, I sent my Mom a telegram that read, "Start the chicken frying. Be home soon." Fifty years later, she gave me that telegram and I still have it.

While we were in Albuquerque, waiting to get out of the Army Air Force, I drove gas trucks to fuel the B-29's. Every night I had to drive the bus to town and back, but it was a busload of WAC's. It was a tough job, but somebody had to do it.

On the weekends there was always a list of townspeople who would like to have you come out for dinner and (Boy!) there were some darn good cooks and pretty daughters.

The day finally came for me to go home and after boarding the train, I found out there was a flash flood and the railroad tracks were washed out. Everyone had to get off the train and get on a bus that took forever to get to Portland, Oregon.

But nothing lasts forever. Finally I was home and had my feet under my Mom's table. I was one very lucky guy to go through what I did and come home in one piece.

Staff Sergeant Leonard E. Thompson, 18 years old

To: Darrel Roby
    And the Evergreen Aviation Museum
From: Leonard Thompson
Subject: My Appreciation

June 1, 2000

I would like to take the time to send this letter of appreciation to Darrel Roby, his pilot, crew and the Evergreen Aviation Museum for my trip down "memory lane" when I was allowed to take a flight on their B-17 Flying Fortress from Portland.

As we sat there preparing for the take-off with those engines belching black smoke, it was a lot more noisy than I remembered, but of course I wasn't wearing the helmet we wore in World War II.

After we were airborne (being an old tail-gunner) I couldn't resist crawling back and taking a look from the tail. It was just like the old days when I made my way on my hands and knees. The co-pilot had to see just how much he could shake the back part of the plane (just kidding) and I squatted down on the seat and ran through my mental checklist. Things were missing, though, and only the guns were in place and they weren't loaded with live ammunition. There was no place to plug in my oxygen mask, the throat mike, and even the relief tube was missing (but it was hard to use back there anyway).

But, looking out the tail really brought back some memories. I saw a few people on the ground waving at us and it made me feel really good.

As I let my mind wander, I remembered the flight on 3 February, 1945. It was very early in the morning and a flashlight was poked under my nose to wake me up. As I got dressed, I wondered if today was the day my number was up.

The crew and I climbed into a lorry filled with our gear and we headed to the mess hall for a breakfast of powdered eggs and hotcakes. Then we were back to the briefing room and looking at the curtain that covered the screen and hid our secret mission for the day.

When the curtain was raised we got to see maps of today's planned route and what the weather was supposed to be like, and then the target, which was Berlin, which always had plenty of flak and fighter plane protection.

After the briefing, we were back into the lorries and heading for our plane, which the ground crew had already prepared. The engines were warming up as we boarded and waited for the tower to shoot a flare to tell us we could take off.

Today we were the lead crew, the first to take off. As we took off down the runway, the rest of the group was very close behind us, only seconds apart as we headed across the English Channel.

As we kept climbing, I looked back to count the planes and all thirty-six were there. I told the pilot everything was okay and he said, "Alright, lets go to work" and he gave the engines more throttle and we continued our climb.

At this point, we were going through a cloud layer and when we topped out, it looked like a motorboat skimming over the water. The co-pilot came on the radio and said it's time to put on our oxygen masks on and check our guns. So we all fired a round or two to make sure the guns are okay, but I never had a malfunction.

We were now heading over enemy territory and everyone was keeping a watchful eye. We were flying at 26,500 feet and the temperature was minus 47 degrees. The moisture from my oxygen mask made frozen icicles all over me and all the way down my lap. It was important to remember that you don't dare touch any metal with bare skin or you would leave the skin where you touched.

The top turret called out, "Bandits at one o'clock high," and the shooting began. But, in the tail you didn't pick them up until about 4 o'clock high and by that time the fighter plane was in a pursuit curve and I had him in my sights. He managed to slip away, though. But, another Me109 came up, and we were all shooting and we saw black smoke and flames coming from his plane and he was gone.

Even with all the guns shooting at him, you just knew that it's your shot that that got him, but who can really tell.

Now the 109's were gone and we were approaching our bomb run. The air was filled with flak. The group tightened and the bombardier was in charge now. The bomb bays would open and because we were the lead plane, our bombardier shot a flare when we dropped our bombs. Then all the other planes did the same and a whole lot of destruction was on its way.

Back in the tail I could see the bombs hit because the clouds had disappeared. The Bomb Bay closed and it was time to find our way home. That's the time the 109's liked to pick on the B-17's that were in bad shape, but a few P-51 Mustangs are waiting to escort us and the 109's were scared of them.

Our wing man lost two engines and he was too far from base so he headed to Russia and was escorted by a Russian fighter (we heard after the war). We checked to see if anyone was hurt and there was no answer from the radio operator. The waist gunner checked on him and he was shot up pretty bad. We had no trouble on the way back with those P-51's cruising around.

Finally, we were back over the English Channel again and our oxygen masks were off. The white cliffs of Dover were sure a welcome sight. Our base was in sight and we fired a red flare to let ground control know we had "wounded aboard." That gave us priority in landing with an ambulance following us to our pad.

That was the radio operator's last flight. After landing, we counted the holes in the plane and there were 127 of them. Two of the holes were big enough for me to crawl through and they were only inches from the gas tank.

We gathered up our gear, got into the back of a lorry, and we were on our way back to the hut to clean up.

Then on to the mess hail to fill up again since we all missed lunch a long time ago. Sitting in the tail for over eight hours and having the oxygen on most of the time makes a person very tired.

After eating, we would check the bulletin board to see if we were up tomorrow. If not, we would get a good night's sleep.

The ground crew had a lot of work to do, patching all those holes, cleaning out the empty shell casings, and reloading with live ones. Everyone has a job to do.

When you are 18 years old you grow up fast and you only look ahead for the next flight.

Once again, please accept my sincere thanks for that walk through memory lane.

Leonard Thompson

Making a safe landing at the 401st Bomb Group's airfield at Deenethorpe, England

A Newspaper Clipping:
The Oregon Daily Journal, 1945

Thompson Awarded Medal For Service

Park Place, June 7: Park Place adds another name to its Honor Roll of men receiving medals and awards for courage and valor displayed during World War II.

Staff Sergeant Leonard E. Thompson, son of Mrs. Mayme Thompson, a Clackamas Heights-Park Place resident, has been awarded the Air Medal for ". . . meritorious achievement while serving as a B-17 flying Fortress Tail Gunner in the 401st Bombardment Group, commanded by Lt. Col. W.T. Seawell, of Pine Bluff, Arkansas."

The citation accompanying the award reads, ". . . for exceptional merit and participating in a number of combat bombardment missions over Germany and Nazi-held territory. The courage, coolness, and skill shown by Staff Sergeant Thompson on these occasions reflect the highest credit upon himself and the armed forces of the United States."

Sergeant Thompson is well known in this vicinity. He was born in Oregon City and was reared in the Clackamas Heights-Park Place District. He attended, and was graduated from, Oregon City High School.

Condolences to the widow of a friend

October 9, 2000

Dear Billie,

When your daughter Joy called and told me that Jack had passed away it brought tears to my eyes and I choked all up. I'm sorry I couldn't make arrangements in time for the funeral, but Jack would understand.

We had a lot of great experiences in our short time together. Like the time in Rapid City where (in a lake) we learned how to get out of the B-17 if we ever had to ditch in the water. The lake wasn't deep, but when we jumped off the wing of the plane into the rubber boat it slipped out from under us and we had to fend for ourselves. Jack was a couple inches taller than me and his nose was just out of the water and mine just below water line. As we made our way to shore and crawled out of the lake with me spitting water, he just kept on laughing. He said, "It's a good thing are no alligators in there," and soon we were all laughing.

Another time, when we first arrived at our base overseas, there was an air raid and so like a bunch of wild rabbits we ran for the air raid shelter. Arriving at the door at the same time we were both fighting to be first inside.

Jack's bunk was next to mine and we were very close buddies. I'll bet Jack never told you how we used to wrestle all the time to see who was the best. It turned out to be about 50-50.

We went to London a few times together and did a lot of sight seeing. We would get lost on the subway and had to find our way back to base.

When we were flying we had to put on our oxygen masks above 10,000 feet. Sometimes Jack and I would take our masks off at 20,000 feet and wrestle for a minute and would be all out of breath, but we would take a shot of pure oxygen and feel great again.

We did a lot of growing up in a hurry and were very lucky at being in the right place at the right time.

I am so sorry that Jack has passed on, but wherever he is I'm sure he will have that smile on his face and be awaiting our arrival. Jack was a very special friend.

Jack's old Tail Gunner,

Leonard

Back from Hamburg over the Rhine River.

Meaning of the Oak Leaf Clusters and The Orange and Blue Ribbons

The blue and orange ribbon is the Air Medal, which is given for Meritorious Achievement while participating in a number of Combat missions over Germany and Nazi held territories.

The Courage, coolness and skill shown by Staff Sergeant Thompson on these Occasions reflect the highest credit upon himself and the Armed forces of the United States.

The Oak Leaf Clusters show how many times he has won this citation.

The Blue Ribbon on the right side of the jacket is for his Bomb Group, the 401st for outstanding performance and bombing accuracies on targets of high risk, and the Oak Clusters the same.

The Red and White ribbon is for being a "good boy."

The beautiful B-17 in flight.

Among Leonard's souvenirs was this anonymous piece. It must have had special meaning for him.

There I was alone in a pub, sipping a cold one, thinking of dead buddies. I was watching the girls and their playboy dates, drinking and having fun, wondering if even they knew a war was going on.

A sweet young thing, on the tipsy side, glanced up from her glass of port and seeing me alone and sad, figured she'd have some fun. "Look at the handsome flyer, girls," she said. "I saw him first. He's mine. Look at the cute uniform and all those ribbons!"

"Tell me about yourself," she said. "What do the ribbons mean? What's the one on the left, and those stars? What do they mean?"

I was embarrassed and angry, too. I got up to go but a sailor nearby said "I'll tell her, mate. It's damn near time she knew."

This is what he said:

"The ribbon itself is the E.T.O. (European Theater of Operations) and each color means something special. The Brown is for the sand of the desert, the Green for the English fields, the Black is for the color of Germany and the White and Red is for France. The three strips down the center are all for the Yankee dead. The stars (four of them) are of major engagements and battles he's seen."

"The first star is for the air offensive in Europe, but it has much more meaning. It's the flak, the fighters and for comrades lost. It's for fighting your way to the target against everything the Jerries threw at us and for watching your buddies being shot from the sky and going down in twisting flame."

"The second star is for the Normandy campaign and all of it's blood and gush D-Day. It's the men we left on Omaha Beach and the dead who paved the way. It's the LST's and LSD's (landing crafts for troops and

equipment) we left on the beach. It's for the mines that exploded and the bodies of the first young kids who tried to get ashore. It's the broken and fallen B-17's that burned in the fields of France. The B-17's dropped their load of bombs on the Jerry lines and gave our troops a chance."

"The third star is for the fight in Northern France right up to the Siegfried Line. It's for the paratroopers hanging on cruel barbed wire and the filthy SS swine. It's for the glider troops far behind the lines who were slaughtered with out a chance. It's for the blood and guts of the infantry spilled on the fields of France. It's for the burned out tanks, the slime, the mud, and the shrapnel from bursting shells.

"The fourth star is for Germany and the awful toll we paid and for the kid next door who died. It's for the prison camps and the stinking food, the land mines, and the missing foot. It's for the brave young kid with his arm half gone, who smiles at you, smokes a cigarette, and dies."

"What are the stars you ask? They are for the blood, the guts, and the hitch in hell. That's exactly what they mean."

Newspaper clipping from the Oregon Daily Journal

Chapter Two

The 401st Bombardment Group
613th Bomb Squadron

The Crew of: 1st Lt. K.D. Speer

Pilot: 1st Lt. K.D. Speer
Copilot: 2nd Lt. J.J. Kelly
Navigator: 2nd Lt. R.H. Simon
Bombardier: 1st Lt. W.M. Scanlon
"Mickey" Operator (Radar): 2nd Lt. L. Baker
Radio Operator: T/Sgt. D. Yohay
Engr/Top Turret: T/Sgt. G.G. Cupp
Ball Turret Gunner: S/Sgt. W.D. Gross
Tail Gunner: S/Sgt. L.E. Thompson
Waist Gunner: S/Sgt. J.C. Averett

Mission	Date	Assigned B-17
1. Berlin	3 Feb 1945	44-6132
2. Giessen	6 Feb 1945	44-6132
3. Nurnburg	20 Feb 1945	44-6132
4. Harburg	24 Feb 1945	43-38607
5. Siegen	7 Mar 1945	44-8708 (PFF & Gee-H Ship)
6. Hagen	10 Mar 1945	44-8653 (PFF Ship)
7. Hopsten	21 Mar 1945	44-6947
8. Barmingholten	22 Mar 1945	44-6947
9. Rheine	24 Mar 1945	44-6947
10. Unterluss	4 Apr 1945	43-38941
11. Royan	15 Apr 1945	44-8454 (PFF & Gee-H Ship)

The 401st Bombardment Group
A short Historical Chronology

Two Distinguished Unit Citations
Best bombing accuracy record among B-17 groups in the Eighth Air Force
Second lowest loss ratio among B-17 groups in the Eighth Air Force
First group in the ETO to complete 100 combat missions in seven months
Combat missions: 254
Accredited sorties: 7,413
Percentage of aircraft available for each mission: 95.6%
Aircraft lost on operational missions: 94
Aircraft returning with battle damage: 1,872
Total personnel entering enemy territory: 69,910
Total battle casualties (KIA, MIA, wounded): 1,078
Tons of bombs dropped (all targets): 17,784
Rounds of ammunition fired: 916,920
Enemy aircraft claimed (confirmed): 193
Individual awards and decorations: 11,884

Missions:
001 to 100 (26 Nov '43 - 25 Jun '44)
101 to 200 (28 Jun '44 - 28 Jan '45)
201 to 254 (29 Jan '45 - 20 Apr '45)

Combat Aircraft and Air Crews
612th Squadron (SC)
613th Squadron (IN)
614th Squadron (IW)
615th Squadron (IY)

Support Units at Station 128
450th Sub Depot
78th Station Complement
379th Service Squadron
861st Chemical Company

1199th Military Police Company - Photo
1209th Quartermaster Service Group
2966th Finance Detachment
860th Chemical Company
18th Weather Detachment

Chronology of Group Bombardment Events

18-October-1943: The Group departed Great Falls for the England. The ground echelon went by way of Camp Shanks, New York, then (in the dead of night) to New York City where they boarded the Queen Mary, and arrived at the Firth of Clyde on 2 November. The air echelon flew various routes, typical of which was by way of Scott Field, on to Goose Bay, Labrador, followed by Meeks Field, Iceland, and finally to Prestwick, Scotland.

26-November-1943: The first combat mission'starget was Bremen, Germany. Colonel Bowman commanded the 401st in the lead aircraft. In terms of numbers, this was the largest mission the Eighth Air Force had thus far sent to Germany.

1-December-1943: Second combat mission, led by Lt. Colonel Harris E. Rogner, Deputy Group Commander. The Group received credit for downing its first enemy aircraft.

5-December-1943: B-17 piloted by Lt. Walter B. Keith crashed on take-off into the Village of Deenethorpe. All members of the crew escaped from the airplane and alerted residents of Deenethorpe before the plane exploded. Although most of the buildings in the village were severely damaged, no lives were lost.

20-December-1943: The Group formally assumes control of Station 128, which was previously an RAF training base.

24-December-1943: Enlisted men at the base entertained 650 English children at a Christmas party in the mess halls, with plenty to eat!

30-December-1943: The Group suffered its first

loss of a crew, that of Lt. Trian Neag, on a mission to Ludwigshaven.

31-December-1943: Two 401st aircraft were lost in an attack on Cognac Airdrome, Lt. Colonel I.W. Eveland, commander of the 614th Squadron, parachuted safely and subsequently escaped from France by walking over the Pyrenees Mountains into Spain.

January-1944: The Group was commended by the Commanding General of the 94th Combat Wing for the accuracy of its bombing and its efficiency in adapting to Eighth Air Force procedures.

11-January-1944: The 401st led the combat wing on what has been termed "the greatest air battle of WW II." The Group encountered fierce enemy aircraft resistance, in which it was supported by Colonel James Howard, a P-51 pilot, who single-handedly fought off 30 Nazi fighters, destroying four, and for which he was awarded the Congressional Medal of Honor. For this mission, the First Air Division, including the 401st, received the Presidential Citation.

20-February-1944: For its performance on a mission to Leipzig, the Group was singled out for the award of its second Presidential Citation.

6-March-1944: The 401st flew its first mission to Berlin, led by Lt. Colonel Edwin Brown, followed by its second mission to Berlin two days later, led by Lt. Colonel D. E. Silver.

1-April-1944: The Group celebrated its first anniversary at a banquet attended by the Commanding Generals of the 1st Air Division and the 94th Combat Wing. A musical revue, "*You Can't Miss It,*" was staged and produced by members of the 401st.

13-April-1944: The Group, led by Lt. Colonel D.E. Silver, participated in the costly raid on the ball bearing works at Schweinfurt, losing two crews.

24-May-1944: After bombing Berlin, Lt. John S. Whiteman's crew crash landed in Denmark, where they "procured" some boats, rowed to Sweden and eventually returned safely to England.

28-May-1944: On a mission to Dessau, the Group suffered its heaviest loss on a single mission. The 401st was singled out for attack by 200 enemy aircraft and as a result lost six crews, while a seventh ditched in the English Channel.

June-1944: During June the 401st was recognized as having set a new record for bombing accuracy among all groups in the Eighth Air Force, having placed 73 percent of all bombs within 1,000 feet and 96 percent within 2,000 feet of the aiming point.

6-June-1944: The Group participated in the massive Eighth Air Force effort to support the D Day landing in Normandy

12-June-1944: A defective fragmentation bomb being unloaded by the armament section of the 614th Squadron exploded, killing seven men and badly injuring eleven others.

25-June-1944: The Group completed its 100th mission, which was celebrated the following day by a hanger party featuring beer and hot dogs. The Group was commended by the Commanding General of the 1st Air Division for being the first Group in the European Theater of Operations (ETO) to complete 100 missions within seven months.

8-August-1944: On a mission to the Caen area, the lead aircraft of the 401st was shot down. While five members of the crew bailed out, the ball turret gunner was unable to extricate himself, and because of a pre-arranged pact, four members of the crew crashed with the ship in what was one of the strongest bonds of friendship ever recorded in the ETO.

28-September-1944: The Group completed its 150th mission.

September-1944: The 401st Fliers, the Group's crack softball team, won the American Red Cross invitational meet at Northampton and were generally regarded as ETO champions.

15-November-1944: The Group celebrated its first year of operations, during which it flew 172 missions, the 172nd being to Merseburg.

5-December-1944: Colonel Bowman was called to Headquarters of the United States Air Force in Europe as Deputy Chief of Staff to General Carl Spaatz and was succeeded as group commander by Colonel William T. Seawell, the Deputy Commanding Officer.

19-to-26-December-1944: During what became known as the "Battle of the Bulge," the Group flew a mission to Schleiden, after which the entire group was diverted to an RAF airbase near Land's End in southwestern England because of dense fog at Deenethorpe. The Group flew another mission from that point but was again diverted upon returning to England. Not until December 26, an absence of a week for 32 crews, did all airplanes return to Deenethorpe.

28-January-1945: For its 200th mission, the Group flew to Cologne, led by Lt. Colonel William C. Garland. During January, the 401st completed 30 consecutive missions without loss of a crew.

1-February-1945: A party in the form of a carnival-circus was held in Hanger No. 1 to celebrate the 200th mission. Among the guests were Lt. General James H. Doolittle, Commanding General of the Eighth Air Force, and the commanding generals of the 1st Air Division and 94th Combat Wing

February-1945: The Group closed the month by flying thirteen consecutive missions in thirteen days.

March-1945: A new record of twenty-two missions in a month was set, which included 754 sorties. During the month the Group encountered its first Nazi jet fighters.

20-April-1945: The 401st flew its 254th and last mission, targeting Brandenberg. The Group received the 94th Combat Wing Best Bombing Plaque for its record in March.

8-May-1945: VE Day meant the end of hostilities in Europe and a permanent stand-down of the 401st Bomb Group, which was celebrated by a huge fireworks display. Formal ceremonies were held the following day.

May-1945: The Group flew three low level flights over the Ruhr Valley for ground personnel to enable them to observe the results of aerial bombing. Also, the 401st made four trips to Linz, Austria, to evacuate French and British prisoners of war.

15-May-1945: A Field Order was received stating that the 401st was to be moved immediately to the United States.

30-May-1945: The first of 78 aircraft, piloted by Colonel Seawell, departed from Deenethorpe for the United States, landing at Valley in Wales, Iceland and Goose Bay, Labrador, before touching down at Bradley Field, Massachusetts.

20-June-1945: A series of trains loaded with ground personnel departed from Geddington Station for Gurock, Scotland, where they boarded the Queen Elizabeth for the voyage home, leaving the Firth of Clyde on 25 June.

29-June-1945: The Queen Elizabeth docked in New York harbor to receive the greatest welcome ever extended to any ship in the history of the city.

July-1945: After thirty days leave, members of the Group reported to the air base at Sioux Falls, South Dakota, where it was announced that the 401st, like other Eighth Air Force units, was to be deactivated. Members were assigned to new B-29 groups formed for the war against Japan or were held at Sioux Falls awaiting new orders.

2-September-1945: The surrender of Japan

Chapter Three

A Brief History of the Boeing B-17 Flying Fortress

A total of 12,700 planes were produced. The airplane entered service in 1939.

In 1934, the Army issued specifications for a "multi" engine bomber, which Boeing interpreted as four engines. While the Martin B-10 bomber seemed adequate at the time to defend the continental United States, with great foresight Boeing designed an altogether heavier, faster, higher-flying, and longer-range bomber, which proved to be invaluable in the strategic air battles over Germany.

Boeing started design work on its Model 299 in June, 1934. Just over a year later the first flight of the prototype took place at Boeing Field, July 28, 1935.

A month later, the silver aircraft flew to Wright Field, Ohio in record time, but crashed disastrously at its USAAC evaluation flight in October. Despite this accident, which was traced to human error (not a design flaw), the Air Corps recognized the potential of the Model 299 (aka XB-17), and ordered thirteen service-test models (Y1B-17) for evaluation. Among the notable changes incorporated into the Y1B-17 was a 930-hp Wright Cyclone engine, which replaced the original 750-hp Pratt & Whitney engines.

In the 1930's, the nation's military leaders debated bomber doctrine strenuously. Among the most influential views were those of Billy Mitchell and his bomber advocates. For them, the B-17 was a godsend. It was the manufactured, tangible embodiment of a "Flying Fortress."

As early as 1937, the 2nd Bombardment Group was equipped with B-17s, using them to perfect techniques of high-altitude, long-distance bombing. Since the only foreseeable use of such a capability was the defense of the nation's shores from enemy fleets, the U.S. Navy fiercely opposed the Army's development of the four-engine bomber. By way of a compromise the Army ordered 39 more B-17B's. The Army Air Corps' air doctrine envisioned large formations of fast, high-flying B-17 bombers, defending themselves against enemy fighters with their own massed machine-gun fire. Fighter escorts were initially considered impractical and even undesirable by the bomber advocates. Any admission that fighter escort was necessary would imply that enemy fighters posed a real threat and that the Flying Fortresses were not invulnerable.

More improvements followed in the B-17C. More machine guns, self-sealing fuel tanks, more armor plating, and up-rated engines, to name a few. Even though all these increased the weight of the "C" model to 49,650 pounds, the installation of the 1,200 Wright Cyclones made the "C" capable of 320 MPH, the fastest of all B-17 variants.

The B-17D was a slightly modified B-17C, with different engine cowling flaps and an extra pair of machine guns, bringing its total armament to six .50 caliber and one .30 caliber machine guns. Although only 42 of the "D" models were built, by the time of Pearl Harbor the existing "C" models had been upgraded to "D" specifications.

The first B-17D flew on February 3, 1941. Most were sent to Hawaii and the Philippines.

The B-17E model introduced significant changes from the earlier versions, the most visible being the addition of a dorsal fin forward of the now-larger tail, greatly thickening the profile view of the "E" model and later versions when compared to earlier models. These features increased flight stability, especially during high-altitude bomb runs.

Equally significant was the addition of a pair of .50 caliber machine guns in a tail turret, resolving a deficiency that had been noted by August, 1940 when the B-17E was ordered. The addition of the tail turret required a completely redesigned rear fuselage, resulting in a six-foot longer aircraft. The third big change was the installation of powered turrets in the ventral and dorsal positions.

The crew of the B-17E consisted of pilot, copilot, bombardier, navigator, flight engineer, radio operator, Tail Gunner, belly gunner, and two waist gunners. The navigator or bombardier used the nose gun, and the flight engineer operated the dorsal turret.

Using the original 1200 hp engines, these add-ons made for a somewhat slower, but eminently more defensible, B-17E. Its specifications were similar to the B-17D, but the overall length was 74 feet, and it carried nine machine guns (eight .50's and one .30). Boeing produced 512 "E" models.

The B-17F was the first B-17 variant to be produced by all of the "B.V.D." companies (Boeing, Lockheed/Vega, and Douglas). Because of the pressing demand for the Flying Fortress, Boeing provided blueprints and cooperation for the B-17 to be built at the Douglas plant in Long Beach and the Vega plant in Burbank. Altogether, they would turn out 3405 B-17Fs: 2300 by Boeing, 605 by Douglas, and 500 by Lockheed/Vega. The first B-17F flew in May, 1942.

From the outside, the "F" closely resembled the "E." Only the unframed, bubble-style Plexiglas nose seemed to be different. Internally, however, more than 400 changes made the B-17F a better bomber. Changes such as the new Wright R-1820-97 Cyclone engines (capable of 1380 hp in short bursts), paddle-bladed propellers, a stronger undercarriage, external bomb racks, better brakes, carburetor intake filters, etc.

B-17F's participated in the January 27, 1943 raid on Wilhelmshaven, the first USAAF mission over Germany. The Luftwaffe pilots quickly identified the B-17's vulnerability to head-on attack. Field modifications, typically jury-rigged machine guns, didn't help much. The stage was set for the B-17G, the definitive variant of the Flying Fortress.

The B-17G fairly bristled with defensive firepower. It had 13 Browning .50 caliber machine guns and the chin, dorsal, ventral, and tail turrets each mounted a pair of guns (8). Left- and right-side guns in the cheeks and waist added 4 more guns and a single, rear-firing gun on the top of the fuselage made 13. No wonder Luftwaffe pilots suffered from "vier motor schreck" ("four-engine fear").

The most distinctive change was the "chin" turret, sticking out below the nose. It looks like an after-thought, and it was. But the two machine guns there addressed the B-17's earlier vulnerability.

With 8,680 produced between July 1943 and April 1945, the "G" was the most numerous B-17 variant: 4,035 B-17Gs by Boeing, 2,395 by Douglas, and 2,250 by Lockheed/Vega. The vast majority of surviving B-17s are model "G's".

The Eighth Air Force (8AF) was organized in England in early 1942. Its mission was to destroy Germany's ability to wage war, through daylight bombing raids (complementing the RAF's nighttime attacks). Massed formations of Flying Fortresses would eventually roam all over Occupied Europe, wreaking havoc on the German war machine, while relying on the bombers' speed, altitude, and its inherent firepower for protection.

Billy Mitchell, "Boom" Trenchard, and Guilio Douhet were finally proven to be correct in their doctrine of bombardment.

The first B-17E arrived in Britain on July 1, 1942. Six weeks later, August 17, eighteen Flying

Fortresses launched their first raid against Nazi Europe, hitting rail yards at Rouen. Eighth Air Force head General Ira Eaker went along on this mission, flying in Yankee Doodle; the Luftwaffe didn't come up that day. Light opposition continued for the next ten missions.

On January 27, 1943, for the first time, American bombers hit inside of Germany itself, the submarine facilities at Wilhelmshaven.

A turning point in the war was reached on April 17, when 115 Flying Fortresses bombed the Focke-Wulfe factory in Bremen. As if defending its nest, the Luftwaffe struck hard, knocking down sixteen B-17's (a 15 percent loss rate on a single mission). Soon, ten-to-fifteen percent losses became the norm, as the Luftwaffe improved their tactics, in particular by attacking the B-17's head on. Thus the famous phrase "Bandits at twelve o'clock high!"

In late 1943, P-38's and P-47's began to provide the long range escorting that the "Forts" needed. But the ultimate answer, the P-51 Mustang, which could reach as far as Berlin, only appeared in March, 1944.

In February, 1944, and especially in the third week, later dubbed "The Big Week," the Eighth Air Force launched massive raids against German aircraft manufacturing in Leipzig, Augsburg, Regensburg, Schweinfurt, Stuttgart, etc.

Starting on the 20th, VIII Bomber Command launched over 1,000 Flying Fortresses in an attempt to destroy the Luftwaffe. American losses were heavy: 244 bombers and 33 fighters, but the Luftwaffe's strength never recovered. Its losses in the air were almost as damaging as the destruction of the factories.

During the month of March 1944, Mustangs escorted the B-17s all the way to Berlin. When Air Marshal Goering saw Mustangs over Berlin, he knew all was lost for the Third Reich. From that date forward, the bombers could range all over Germany at will. Although they were not immune from losses, the fighter escorts would keep the Allied losses down and to continue to erode the Luftwaffe's strength.

While tangential to the B-17 story, Germany's inadequate pilot training and its short-sighted non-rotation of pilots made it impossible for the Luftwaffe to make good its losses, while competently trained American aircrew filled, replaced, and expanded the 8AF roster continuously.

With D-Day n June, the Eighth Air Force flew 23 missions, mostly against tactical targets, airfields, and marshalling in northern France. These missions included 800 sorties, with only nine planes lost. In the last five months of 1944, the 457th ran 87 missions, about 2700 sorties (540 per month), and lost 66 planes (13 per month), for a monthly loss ratio of 2.5 percent. Losses were higher than earlier in the year, but far below the unbearable experience of 1943

B-17 on display at the Evergreen Aviation Museum in McMinnville, Oregon. This is very similar to the type of bomber Leonard flew during his World War II missions.

Right up to the bitter end in May, 1945, the B-17 Flying Fortresses continued to batter the Third Reich. More than any other airplane, the big Boeing bombers brought the war to the Germans and won.

Pictures of Me262 Jet Fighers taken by B-17 photographers. Leonard was one of the first to see these new airplanes.

Chapter Four

An Informal Photo Album

Leonard prior to enlisting in the army.

Deenthorpe, England
Home of the 401st Bombardment Group's Base

Deenethorpe Castle

Deenethorpe Church

Deenethorpe Farmer

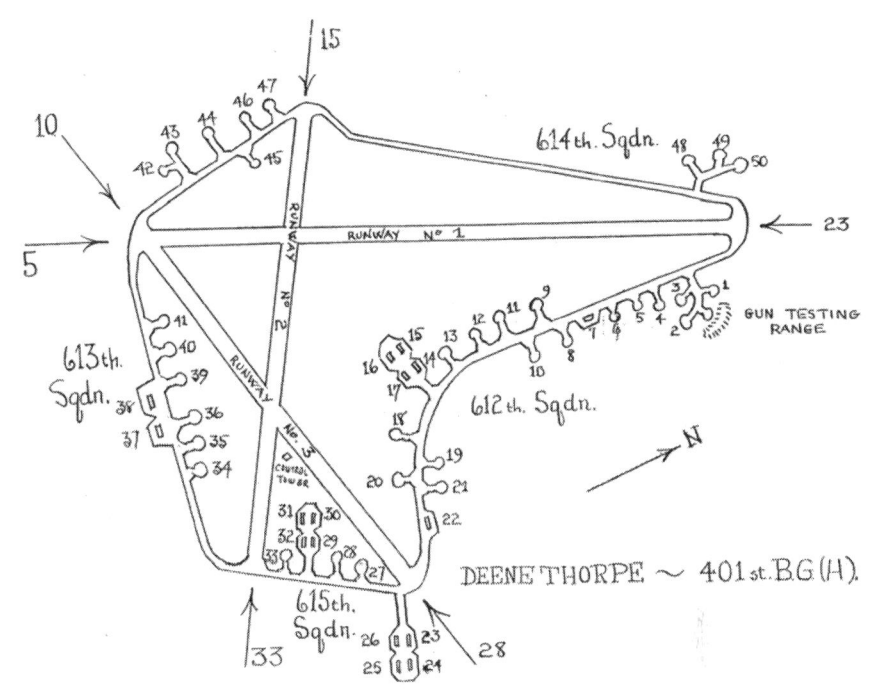

Assigned parking for the 401st Bomb Group

Boeing B17 "Liberty Belle"

"I saw this happen to a good friend. What a helpless feeling"
S/Sgt. Leonard Thompson

THE CITY OF BERLIN UNDER ATTACK FROM THE AIR ON FEBRUARY 3, DURING THE GREAT DAYLIGHT ASSAULT BY 1,000 AMERICAN FLYING FORTRESSES which brought indescribable chaos to the German capital, where 3,000,000 refugees are trying to find shelter

Berlin has long been a target for Allied bombers; yet it is doubtful if any previous raid has wrought so much havoc in the German capital as that carried out on Saturday last in daylight. One thousand American "heavies," escorted by large numbers of fighters, dropped "one bomb carpet after another" (as a neutral correspondent described it), and left the city in flames as a result of the 2,500 tons of high-explosives and incendiaries which they delivered. This attack came at a moment when some 3,000,000 refugees from the eastern parts of Germany were crowded into Berlin, in addition to its normal residents. The very heart of the city was the target, and reports have given a terrifying summary of the results: it is now known, for instance, that eight direct hits were scored on the Air Ministry building, and that eighteen concentrations of high-explosives covered the area occupied by the War Office, the Reich Chancellery, Ministry of Propaganda, the Gestapo Headquarters, Ministry of Agriculture and other important buildings. The American bombers swept over the capital in two waves, and in forty-five minutes had delivered the heaviest attack yet made by our Allies. The picture reproduced here shows, in the upper left-hand corner, the Tempelhof airfield, on which bombs are actually falling; lower down on the left are the marshalling yards feeding the Potsdamer and Anhalter stations

Bombing the marshalling yards in Luxembourg

Barely making it back to base only to crash.

A B-17 ground crew loads bombs for the next mission

401st Bomb Group "Bowman's Bombers"

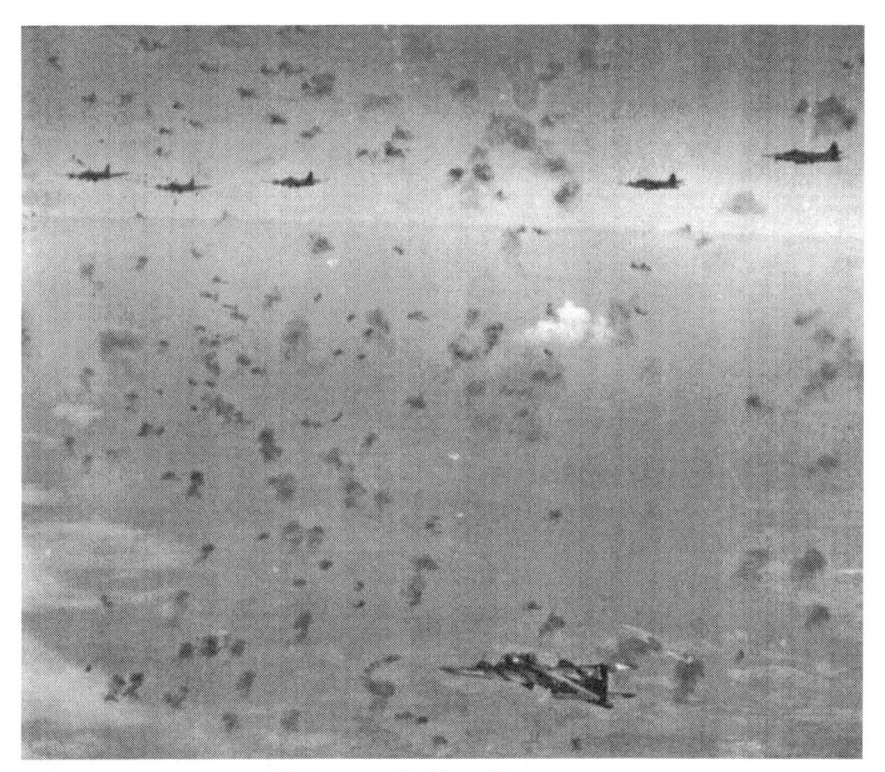

Flak over Politz, Germany

The 401st Bomb Group runway at Deenethorpe, England during their 50th reunion. Gertrude is riding in the jeep that Leonard rode in during World War II

Leonard's first crew: *Top row:* Charles Bennett; pilot, John Wild; Bombadier, Albert Lundberg; co-pilot, Floyd Henderson; Waist Gunner, Leonard Thompson; Tail Gunner, James Lundy; Navigator. *Bottom Row:* Eddie Kieper; Ball Turrett Gunner, Sherman Spencer; Waist Gunner. Six bailed out and were never seen again. Lt. Bennett died when their plane exploded after crashing. Leonard was the sole survivor

Lt. Speer's Crew in 1945.
Leonard is in the middle of the front row

Aerial map of Leipzig power station, a prime bombing target.

SECOND AIR FORCE
GUNNERS FLYING TRAINING REPORT

Thompson, Leonard E.	Cpl	39342184	I-53
Name	Rank	ASN	Crew Number

9-29-44	AAB RC, SD		AAB RC, SD
Date Crew Activated	Group	Squadron	Station

Total Flying Time　　　　　　Previous Schools Attended - Dates
Prior to First Phase

FIRST PHASE

9-29-44	AAB RC, SD	10-28-44
Date Assigned	Station	Date Transferred to Second Phase

1. Number Air-to-Ground Malfunction Missions /
2. Number Times Operated Ball Turret 2-0
3. Number Times Operated Upper Turret 2-0
4. Proficient Checks Completed YES
5. Total Time in Assigned A/C at this Station 48:45

SECOND AND THIRD PHASE

10-28-44	AAB RC, SD	12-23-44
Date Assigned	Station	Date Transferred to Processing Station

1. Number of Air-to-Ground Malfunction ?
2. Number of Air-to-Air Tow Missions above 20,000 feet 2
3. Number of Rounds Fired above 20,000 feet 390
4. Number of An Gun Camera Missions (Fighter) 2
5. Feet of Film Used in Camera Missions 130
6. Air-to-Air Score on 4 ft. X 20 ft. Target 0
7. Total Time over 20,000 feet 68:10
8. Total Time in Assigned A/C at this Station 165:20

Pertinent remarks by the instructor of this crew member will be noted on back

```
                    THIS IS NOT AN APPLICATION FORM

        IF YOU EXPECT TO APPLY FOR A FAMILY ALLOWANCE FILL OUT THIS DATA
        SHEET AND TAKE IT WITH YOU TO THE RECEPTION CENTER FOR YOUR USE.

        You will be given a chance to apply for the family allowance at your Recep-
        tion Center. The information called for on this sheet will be needed in filling
        out an application. Be sure it is correct and complete. Check all dates, etc.,
        with your dependents. With this information you will then be prepared to make for-
        mal application without delay. You may apply for your wife, child, or former wife
        divorced to whom alimony is payable, or for your dependent parent, brother, sister,
        or grandchild, under certain conditions (see other side of page). Take required
        documentary proof with you to Reception Center (see other side of page).

        Your name    Thompson              Leonard                39,342,184
                    (last name)           (first name)         (ARMY SERIAL NUMBER)
        Your home address  Route 3, Box 371, Oregon City, Oregon

                         WIFE, CHILD, OR FORMER WIFE DIVORCED
           Name              Address              Relationship         Date of Birth

        1.
        2.
        3.
        4.
        5.
        Date and place of marriage to present wife
        Date and place of marriage to divorced wife
        Date of divorce              Amount of monthly alimony or support payment decreed
        by court order or legal agreement for former wife divorced, or wife and/or child
        living separate and apart, $         Date alimony or support payment ceases
        19    . Name and location of court

                         PARENT, BROTHER, SISTER, OR GRANDCHILD
           Name              Address              Relationship         Date of Birth
        6.  Mary Agnes Thompson;  Route 3, Box 371, Oregon City,  Mother   April 20, 1906
                    Marilyn
        7.  Ellen/Mary Thompson;          "              "        sister   March 13, 1927
        8.  Patricia Jean Thompson;       "              "        sister   March 29, 1929
        9.  Joanne Adell Thompson;        "              "        sister   Sept. 23, 1930
        10. Frances Marie Thompson        "              "        sister   May 14, 1933
            Shirley Mae Thompson;         "              "        sister   Nov. 6, 1934
                    PERSON OR PERSONS TO WHOM CHECKS SHOULD BE MAILED
        For dependents listed on lines numbered         Name              Address

            Mary Agnes Thompson, mother                 Route 3, Box 371, Oregon City,

                MEMBERS OF IMMEDIATE FAMILY NOW IN MILITARY OR NAVAL SERVICE
           Name        Home Address     Branch of Service    Relationship      Age

            None
```

Leonard's Family Allowance sheet for his mother and five sisters. As his wife Gertrude said, "Leonard always took care of his family."

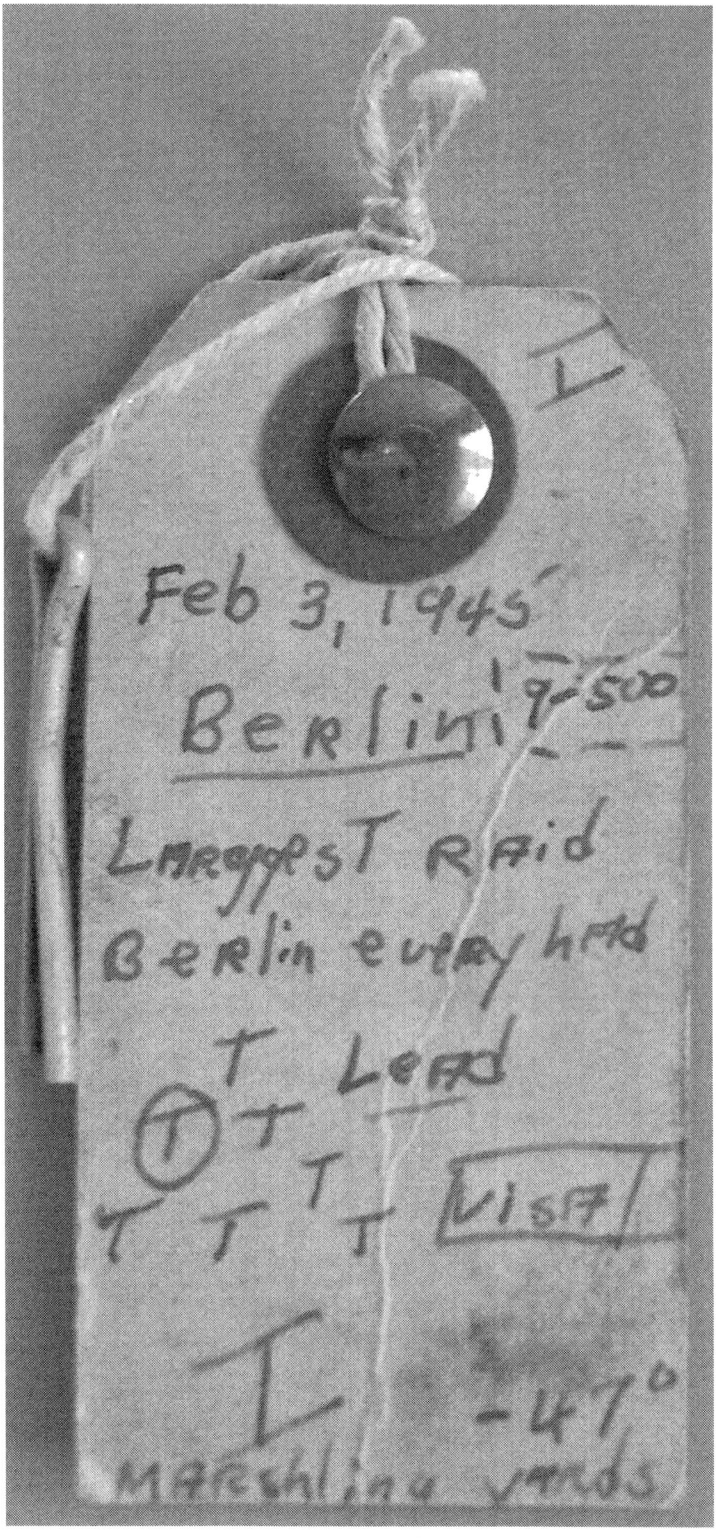
Feb 3, 1945
Berlin
Lead
VISIT
-47°
Marshling yards

Leonard's framed collection: Cotter pins from bombs with information about the bombing run, pictures of bombing runs, and his Eighth Air Force patch.

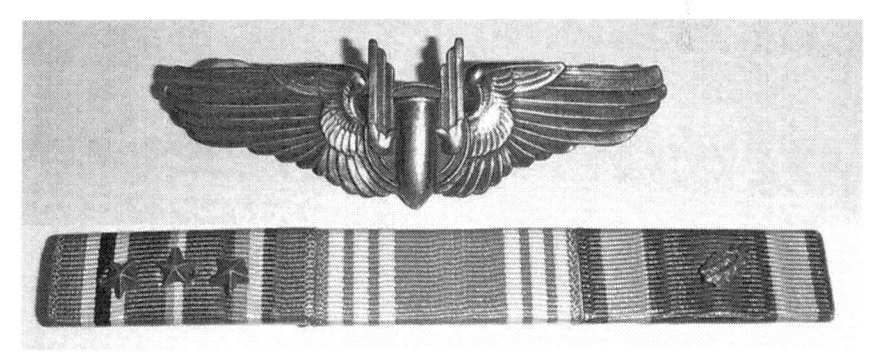

Leonard's Medals:

B17 Bomber Wings
European Theater Ribbon with 3 Stars
Good Conduct Ribbon
Air Medal with Oak Leaf Cluster

INSTRUCTIONS

(1) Learn by heart the Russian phrase "Ya Amerikánets" (*means "I am American" and is pronounced as spelt*).

(2) Carry this folder and contents in left breast pocket.

(3) If you have time before contact with Russian troops, take out the folder and attach it (*flag side outwards*) to front of pocket.

(4) When spotted by Russian troops put up your hands holding the flag in one of them and call out the phrase "Ya Amerikánets."

(5) If you are spotted before taking action as at para 3 do **NOT** attempt to extract folder or flag. Put up your hands and call out phrase "Ya Amerikánets." The folder will be found when you are searched.

(6) You must understand that these recognition aids **CANNOT** be accepted by Soviet troops as proof of bona fides as they may be copied by the enemy. They should however protect you until you are cross questioned by competent officers.

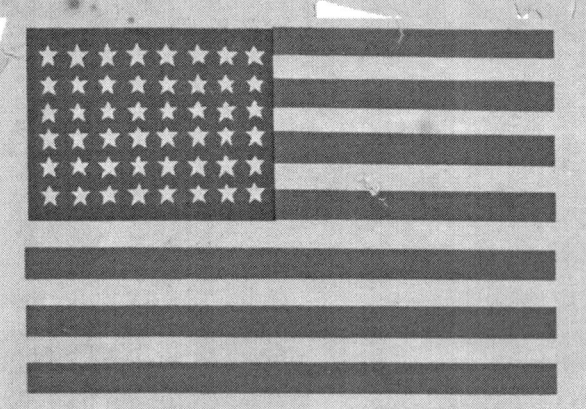

Я американец

"Ya Amerikánets" (*Pronounced as spelt*)

Пожалуйста сообщите сведения обо мне в Американскую Военную Миссию в Москве

Please communicate my particulars to American Military Mission Moscow.

Я американец

"Ya Amerikánets" (*Pronounced as spelt*)

Пожалуйста сообщите сведения обо мне в Американску о Военную Миссию в Москве

Please communicate my particulars to American Military Mission Moscow

Crash Card: to be used if a crew had to crash land in Russia

Leonard's Air Medal

"Jim 401" -- The ceiling of a pub in Cambridge, England. The writing was done by standing on another man's shoulders and was burned with a cigarette lighter. This ceiling is now a historical monument and will never be destroyed.

B-17 Tailgunner's Seat

Deenethorpe in 1995. A much different place than the little farm village of World War II.

401st Bomber Group headquarters at Deenethorpe during the 50th reunion in 1995. The men and their wives visit the shell of the building.

Leonard's leather bomber jacket.
Devastatin' Dody

At Deenethorpe, England for a Reunion. Leonard's wife, Gertrude, sits in the rear on the right. She got to drive up and down the runway where Leonard did takeoffs and landings in the 401st Bombardment Group so many years ago.

Leonard and Gertrude, 1995

Leonard at the 401st Bomber Group Memorial in Deenethorpe,
England during the 50th Anniversary Reunion in 1995. The
monument was built by the local Historical Society
and is a popular tourist attraction.

Leonard in front of a B-17 at the Evergreen Aviation Museum in McMinnville, Oregon. This was the day he flew in a B-17 from Portland to the museum.

Surviving members of Lt. Speer's crew in 1995

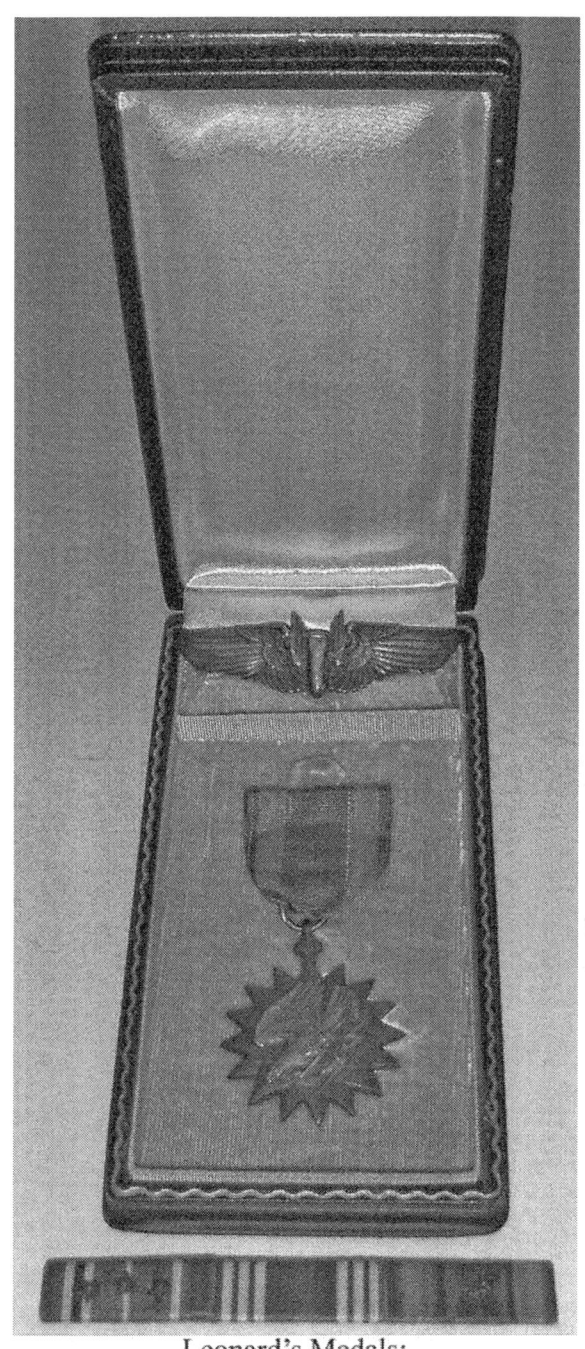

Leonard's Medals:
B17 Bomber Wings and Air Medal
European Theater Ribbon (3 Stars)
Good Conduct Ribbon
Air Medal (Oak Cluster)

Everyone I talked to said Leonard never
said a bad thing about anybody.

21 February, 2005

Leonard E. Thompson died on 21 February, 2005.
He was a hero and he was loved.

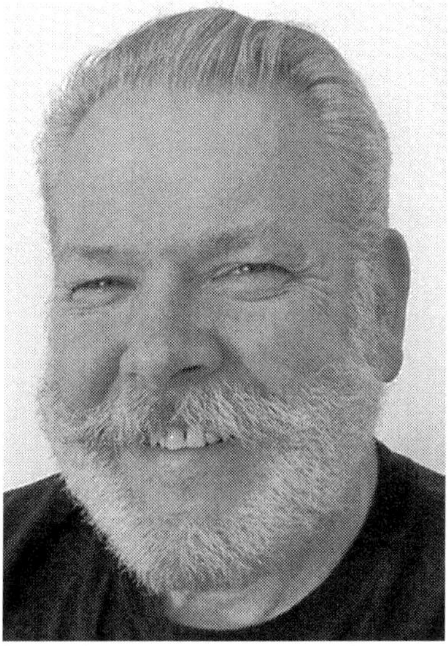

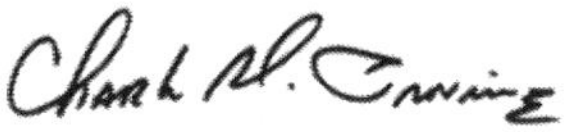

Made in the USA
Charleston, SC
25 May 2012